D0861470

Detail in typography

Letters, letterspacing, words, wordspacing, lines,
linespacing, columns

Hyphen Press · London

Published by Hyphen Press, London,
in 2008
Translated from the German-language
edition published by Verlag Niggli AG,
Sulgen / Zurich, 2005

Text copyright (c) Jost Hochuli, 2008
Translation copyright
(c) Charles Whitehouse, 2008

ISBN 978-0-907259-34-3
www.hyphenpress.co.uk

Contents

Basics

This little book is concerned with those questions of typography that can be considered as belonging to the area of micro- or detail-typography.

While macrotypography – the typographic layout – is concerned with the format of the printed matter, with the size and position of the columns of type and illustrations, with the organization of the hierarchy of headings, subheadings and captions, detail typography is concerned with the individual components – letters, letterspacing, words, wordspacing, lines and linespacing, columns of text. These are the components that graphic or typographic designers like to neglect, as they fall outside the area that is normally regarded as 'creative'.

When reference is made in what follows to formal matters, this does not primarily refer to 'aesthetic' issues in the sense of personal aesthetic freedom or personal taste, but rather to those visible elements that enable the optimum reception of the text. As this is the aim of every piece of typography involving large amounts of text, a concern with formal elements becomes a concern with issues of legibility and readability. Thus, in detail typography, formal elements have little to do with personal preference.

There are many matters of detail typography which one can, in good conscience, resolve differently. The author would certainly not want this book to be regarded as an infallible catechism; rather, he counts on intelligent designers, who, in the spirit of this book, find appropriate solutions to the problems that arise in a given context, even though not all potential problems are dealt with in this text.

And there are texts in which all the details have been attended to – and yet they look so soporifically dull …

The reading process

As experienced readers read, their eyes spring jerkily along the lines. These brief movements are known as saccades, and they alternate with fixed periods lasting 0.2–0.4 seconds. A line is perceived in a series of saccades, followed by a large saccade as the eye jumps back to the left to start the next line. Information is only absorbed during the fixed period. With average type size, as used for books, a saccade represents 5–10 letters, or about 1–2 words in English. A saccade may begin or end within a word. Of the up to 10 letters, only 3–4 are focused on sharply during the fixed period: the rest are perceived by the eye indistinctly and in their context. If the sense of the text is not clear, the eye jumps back, in regression saccades, to recheck what has already been 'read' [1].

The more experienced the reader, the shorter the fixed periods, and the bigger the saccades. If the saccades become too big, and the fixed periods too short – i.e. when one is reading too fast – the text must be guessed at. Here, at least with simple content, the redundancy of language makes comprehension easier. When Jan Tschichold said that it was 'a ridiculous error to think that one can read more quickly', he was obviously wrong, but even with intensive training it is only to a rather limited extent possible to increase one's speed of reading.

Word-images that have already been stored in a reader's visual memory are read more quickly than unfamiliar ones.

It is not yet clear to researchers which signals actually steer the movements of the eye. 'Independently of other external characteristics, the beginnings and ends of lines and of pieces of text are certainly such attributes. They determine the saccades at line changes. Within a line, however, the probability that a particular area will be fixed on is also determined by the sequence of the previous letters or words. In German texts, words with initial capitals are more frequently fixed on than words starting with lowercase letters. The form of the initial letter of a word may also have some slight influence on the probability of fixation. Even with experienced readers, long words cause multiple fixations.'

Apparently, not only the visual structure of the text plays a role in the eye's movements, but also its linguistic structure. 'From which

The circles show points of fixation, on which the eye rests and looks exactly. Straight lines between the circles indicate the saccades (forward jumps), curves indicate the regression-saccades (backward jumps).

1

we may conclude that visual motor activity during reading is also controlled by the language areas of the brain.'

'The registering of eye movements can be used to objectively assess the legibility of a text. The same text will be read at differing speeds if systematic variations are made to the length of line, the size and shape of the type, and the contrast between the colour of the letters and their background. The size and frequency of the saccades depends on the form of the printed text. These variables, which can be measured objectively during the act of reading, correlate very well with the subjective impression of the greater or lesser legibility of a text … .' These researchers confirm – not invariably, but surprisingly frequently – long-known rules of typography.

The letter

Our letters have grown slowly. Over time, they have adapted to various writing techniques and tools, to the materials to be written on, to production techniques and prevailing styles – less in their basic structure than in their details. Changes have mostly occurred unnoticed and over long periods.

The reception of everything written – including typography – takes place in two ways: firstly, in the act of reading itself, that is the conversion in the brain of the perceived succession of letters, and secondly as a (mostly unconscious) visual perception, that triggers associations with what has previously been seen and arouses feelings (see also 'The qualities of type', p. 54).

For this reason, and because typefaces have to meet various demands and fulfil various functions, a particular typeface cannot be described as generally good or bad, useful or useless. Typefaces for continuous text are subject to different criteria than typefaces for headlines on posters and in advertisements, for book jackets or for decorative purposes. Hard-to-read types, used skilfully and sparingly, can catch the attention of the reader or observer – can shock, provoke and thus encourage a closer look and the absorption of the information contained in the other words and pictures. Which typefaces to use, and how to use them for the multitude of advertising tasks that arise, are questions that designers have to answer on a case-by-case basis [2].

Readers of larger amounts of text, and book readers in particular, generally have a conservative attitude to type. They are not in favour of experiments with letters (or other elements of detail typography). These readers are not interested in letters as such. They do not want to look at 'beautiful' or 'interesting' letters, but to understand the meaning of the words they make up. Thus, it is not possible to make significant changes in the form of letters that are used for continuous text. In Stanley Morison's words, they 'will neither be very "different" nor very "jolly"'. It is not a good sign when a layman, reading a book, notices the shape of the letters, and talks of 'noble' or 'modern' letters. All the 'original' and 'noble' special types designed by German type designers (or type 'artists', as they were known) before and after the First World War – some of which were of remarkable quality – were

Italía farà da se

T H E A T R E
M U S I C A L

answer the call

2   None of these types is suitable for large amounts of text. However, if not used too often, they can, in certain contexts, make a fresh and surprising impression. (From top to bottom: ITC Italia Bold; ITC Quorum Black and Light; Goudy Old Style Heavy Face Italic.)

all too 'different', too 'excellent', and are today forgotten. Because the design of their types was too extravagant, and too closely reflected the fashion of the time, many private press and bibliophile editions now look old-fashioned and outmoded [3]. Many of the types designed in our own day will fare no better.

The same fate as befell the romantic, individualistic artists' types of the turn of the century also befell the apparently objective types from the Bauhaus and its adherents, and for the same reason. Here too, form came first – form as such, and not with regard to optimum readability; simplicity of letterform was the ultimate ambition. Furthermore, the type designers focused principally on the isolated individual letters, and less so on letters integrated into words [4]. Paul Renner's Futura has alone outlasted its period in its original freshness. Its success 'was due to the fact that on the one hand it responded to the spirit of the age, i.e. the need for clear "impersonal" forms, but on the other hand, did not deviate too far from familiar letter-

11

Rome, to besiege Ardea, during which siege, the
principall men of the Army meeting one evening
at the tent of Sextus Tarquinius the king's sonne,
in their discourses after supper every one commen-
ded the vertues of his owne wife: among whom
Colatinus extolled the incomparable chastity of

a

Four woodcuts appeared, but the subscribers to
the Review expressed so much disapproval of
these illustrations, conceived and executed in
the uncompromising spirit of Charles Keene's
work, which Mr. Pissarro greatly admired, that
his collaboration was cut short there and then.

b

---

and at what point our impatience with their non-introduction
ought to begin, is always a question. I think we may say safely,
Let them introduce themselves as far as they can contrive to
do it! If they are the true faith of men, all men ought to be
more or less impatient always where they are not found intro-
duced. There will never be wanting Regent-Murrays enough
to shrug their shoulders, and say, "A devout imagination!"
We will praise the Hero-priest rather, who does what is in *him*
to bring them in ; and wears-out, in toil, calumny, contradic-

c

3   The three examples, a, b, c all date from the same period. While the books from
which samples a and b are taken have only collector's value today, and thus represent
no more and no less than art objects in book form, the book from which example c is
taken remains an effective, because functional, and even attractive, object of utility.

With an interest in aesthetics and art history, I may well enjoy the first two books
and their types, but would I also want to read them? The undemanding, 'ordinary' Old
Style type of example c does not attract the reader's attention; no-one perceives its
form as such; it does not force itself between the text and the reader.

a. Golden type by William Morris, from J. DE VORAGINE. *The golden legend*, London: Kelmscott Press, 1892.

b. Brook type by Lucien Pisarro, from T. STURGE MOORE, *Brief account of the origin of the Eragny Press*, London: Eragny Press, 1903.

c. Old Style type, from THOMAS CARLYLE, *Sartor resartus*, London: Chapman &
Hall, 1902.

abcdefghi
jklmnopqr
stuvwxyz

abcdefghi
jklmnopqr
stuvwxyz
a   d ɗ

4   Left: Herbert Bayer's 'Universal-Alfabet', first published in 1926. At right, the semi-bold version of the final design. Reproduced from HANS PETER WILLBERG, *Schrift im Bauhaus / Die Futura von Paul Renner*, Neu-Isenburg, 1969. Assembled into words, the type creates a blobby, hard-to-read impression. The transitions from curves to uprights have not been adjusted optically, and form lumps (see [17] left). The attempt to construct a, b, c, d, e, g, h, n, o, p, q, u, x and y on the basis of a circle of constant diameter results in unusual proportions.

forms. (The excessively different alternative forms for some letters, based wholly on geometric constructions, failed to become established in practice)' [5].

It is almost impossible to define a good, timeless type as such. All that can be done is to point to a few particularly conspicuous characteristics.

The first of these is the familiarity already referred to; the eye of the reader must not be distracted by an unfamiliar form. Then, the letters in the alphabet must all have the same style, but at the same time, each letter must be clearly differentiated from all the others [6].

Like the Cyrillic and Greek alphabets, the roman alphabet also has both capitals and lowercase letters – that is, two fundamentally different forms of letter that must be combined together into a unity if a harmonious type is to result. While the capitals have retained in their basic structure the static, lapidary appearance of inscriptions, the lowercase, developed from them over hundreds of years, shows the dynamic characteristics of flowing handwritten forms, even in their typographic form [7].

The right proportions for capitals and lowercase are a further criterion for a familiar and easily readable book type. The capitals should not deviate too far from their archetype, the capitalis mo-

Radierungen zeitgemäßer Künstler

Radierungen zeitgemäßer Künstler

5   Above: first version of Futura, with special characters. Below: final version (first cast 1928). Reproduced from WILLBERG: *Schrift im Bauhaus / Die Futura von Paul Renner*.

numentalis, the Roman inscriptional letter of the early imperial period [8]. The archetype for the lowercase is the scriptura humanistica, the book hand that was written in the fifteenth and sixteenth centuries, particularly in Italy. Its forms were punched and engraved in steel (with adjustments for technical reasons) by the punchcutters who worked for Sweynheim and Pannartz, Rusch, Jenson, Aldus and others, and thus found their way into book printing [9].

Also important for a book type that is agreeable to read is the proper relationship between capitals and lowercase, in terms of both size and weight. (This is particularly true of German texts, with their (too) many capitals.) So as not to disrupt the overall appearance of a typeface, the capitals should be somewhat lower than the lowercase ascenders [9, 10].

From the work done by the French ophthalmologist Emile Javal in 1878, we know that the eye does not always need to view a whole letter to recognize the individual forms of the roman lowercase: the upper half of the letter is sufficient [11]. Why this is so remains unclear. (It is not simply the case that the upper half of the x-height and the ascenders is more differentiated than the lower half of the x-height and the descenders; the lower halves of a, g, p, q are more strongly differentiated, even in sanserif faces, and those of o, s, v, w, y and z at least equally so.) At all events, we need to take account of this insight. It is reinforced by an experiment by Brian Coe [12].

If the legibility of a typeface did depend solely on differentiation in the design of the upper half of the x-height, this would put most sanserif faces, and particularly those with the simple form of a, at a disadvantage against classic book types [13].

14

Monogramme
Linotype Univers 830 Basic Black

Monogramme
Monotype Bembo Roman

Monogramme
Futura Bold

Monogramme
Meridien Roman

Monogramme
Linotype Univers 830 Basic Black;
the second o and the second m are set
in Futura Bold

Monogramme
Monotype Bembo Roman; the second
o and the second m are set in Meridien
Roman

Monogramme
Futura Bold; the second o and the
second m are set in Linotype Univers 830
Basic Black

Monogramme
Meridien Roman; the second o and
the second m are set in Monotype
Bembo Roman

6   Apparently insignificant differences in shape immediately become obvious in
the design of letters, as, for example, the quality of the curves in the left-hand group
(the manner of deviation from the circle or arc), and in the right-hand group, the
variations in thickness of line, the quality of the curves and the form of the serifs.

A B C D E F G H I J K L M N O P Q R S T U V W X Y Z
a b c d e f g h i j k l m n o p q r s t u v w x y z

C G ç ᴄ ς ς 8 g

7   The basic structure of capitals is static and lapidary; that of lowercase letters is
dynamic. The stages in the change in form from the first to the fifteenth century are
shown using the letter G/g.

Like all two-dimensional shapes perceived by the eye, letters too
are subject to the laws of optics. The decisive element in assessing
their formal qualities is thus not any kind of measuring instrument,
but the healthy human eye. So the following points, which need to be
taken into account in designing type, are better described as optical
facts, rather than optical illusions:

15

8   Roman inscription, capitalis monumentalis, gravestone (detail), beginning of second century AD. (Aquileia, Museo Archaeologico Nazionale; author's photograph.)

et tu reuerſi ſumus;ut de Aetnae incendi-
is interrogaremus ab iis, quibus notum
eſt illa nos ſatis diligenter perſpexiſſe ;ut

tu reuersi sumus; ut de Aetnae incendi-
is interrogaremus ab iis, quibus notum
est illa nos satis diligenter perspexisse; ut

9   Above: humanist minuscule, second half of fifteenth century, Florence (?). The
humanist minuscule was the written archetype for early roman types (1:1 excerpt
from Ms AN II 34, 1r, Basel University Library, with thanks to Martin Steinmann.
Centre: 1:1 excerpt from *Petri Bembi de Aetna ad Angelum Chabrielem Liber*. Venice,
1496. This type was the pattern for Bembo, cut by Monotype in 1929 (below). (Both
illustrations reproduced from *Petri Bembi De Aetna Liber & Pietro Bembo: Der Ätna*,
Verona, 1970.)

Hlf Hlf Hlf Hlf

10   The capitals of many typefaces, and particularly of those designed for continuous text, are (sometimes significantly) lower than the lowercase ascenders. From
left to right: Trinité Roman Condensed 2, Minion Regular, ITC Officina Serif Book,
Scala Sans Regular.

Upper- and Lowercase

Upper- and Lowercase

11   When the upper half of the x-height and the ascenders are covered, it is almost
impossible to decipher the text. If the lower half is covered, it usually remains com-
prehensible.

how much is expendable

abcdefghijklmnopqrstuvwxyz

12   This shows the partial result of an experiment with which Brian Coe attempted
to discover how much of a lowercase letter can be deleted before it becomes unreadable. Here too, it is remarkable how much the emphasis is on the upper half of
the x-height. (From HERBERT SPENCER, *The visible word,* 2nd edn, London 1969.)

quasi papageno   quasi papageno

quasi papageno   quasi papageno

13   The upper halves of a, g and q of the sanserif face (Futura Book) are identical,
so the letters cannot be differentiated in the absence of the lower halves. They also
differ little from p and o. The comparison with the letterforms of Monotype Bembo
is striking.

17

1. For a given height, a circle and a triangle appear smaller than a square. For them to seem to be the same height, they must extend slightly beyond the top and bottom lines [14].

2. The mathematically equal horizontal division of an area produces an upper half that appears larger than the lower half. To produce two halves of apparently equal size, the dividing line must lie above the mathematical centre, in what is known as the optical centre [15].

3. For a given weight of line, a horizontal line appears heavier than a vertical line. To achieve optically balanced verticals and horizontals, which appear to be of the same weight, the horizontal must be somewhat narrower. This applies not only to straight lines but also to curves, which must indeed be somewhat broader at the broadest horizontal point than the corresponding verticals [16]. For optical reasons, right-leaning diagonals must also be somewhat broader, and left-leaning diagonals somewhat narrower than the verticals. Nor are all verticals of equal length equally wide: the more horizontal connections, the narrower the vertical.

4. Where curves intersect with straight lines or with other curves, or where two diagonals meet, lumps will occur, which, unless corrected, will disfigure the letter and make the composition appear blobby [17; see also 4].

5. Small sizes of type need to be proportionally wider than larger sizes. This is an optical requirement that is essential for optimum readability. (We can see this with our own handwriting: the larger the writing, the narrower the individual letters, and vice versa.) This was taken into account by the early punchcutters.

Although the Multiple Master fonts that addressed this problem did not meet with the success expected of them, they did show the way. OpenType fonts already offer possibilities that go beyond those of MM fonts. They should make it possible, in future, for all characters in a typeface to have the right proportions, weight and letterspacing for the size of type. In addition to optical margin adjustments at both ends of the line, further refinements are envisaged, such as variable kerning. This would enable pairs of letters to be spaced somewhat more tightly or loosely – depending on the amount of space available in the line – and also the counters of letters to be inconspicuously adjusted depending on the available space (which Gutenberg practised).

14

15 To the left, the middle horizontal bar is mathematically centred, and optically centred to the right; the intersection to the left is mathematically centred, and optically centered to the right.

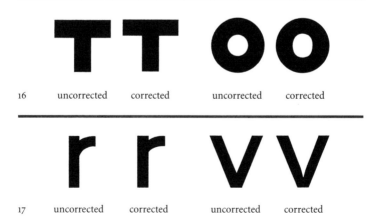

16 uncorrected corrected uncorrected corrected

17 uncorrected corrected uncorrected corrected

The aspects mentioned under 4 and 5 – the formation of lumps and the inadequacy of merely mechanical enlargement or reduction of a typeface – are related to objective and subjective 'radiation'.

Finally, some results of research into the relative legibility of individual letters can be mentioned. The first scientific analyses were published in 1885, with personal observations and subjective impressions already found in 1825. Tinker provides a summary of the results and some conclusions from them:

– Capital A and L are particularly legible, B and Q particularly difficult to discern. B is often confused with R, G with C and O, Q with O, M with W.

– In the lowercase, d, m, p, q are easily legible, j, r, v, x, y averagely legible, and c, e, I, n, l difficult to discern. Lowercase c is often confused with e, I with j, n with a, and l with j.

– Of all the factors governing the relative legibility of lowercase letters, the most important is emphasis on their differentiating characteristics.

Other criteria affecting the appearance and legibility of individual letters are covered in the next chapter, as their effect only becomes apparent within the word.

Something more needs to be said about italic types. Their most obvious characteristic, at first glance, is their slope. In fact, this is only a secondary characteristic. The original written form of our italic types appeared in Florence at the beginning of the fifteenth century, in the same place and at about the same time as the scriptura humanistica. This correspondence hand, which later became known as cancellaresca corsiva, differs structurally from the humanistica in important ways. On average, there are fewer individual pen-strokes, the pen is held at a steeper angle, and the individual letters tend to link together; for a given size, it needs less space as it has leaner proportions. Because for these reasons it can be written relatively quickly, in the hands of many scribes – but by no means all – it acquires a more or less pronounced slope to the right [19].

The first to use italic types in book printing was the Venetian humanist, printer and publisher Aldus Manutius, in 1501, for his 'pocketbook' editions of classical authors [20]. While Aldus and the other printers of the first half of the sixteenth century regarded italic as an independent book type, later on, from the middle of the sixteenth

type sizes fixed quickly margins

a

digitalisierte Typen sind quer

b

Typography is the efficient mean

c

18   Bodoni is not always Bodoni, nor Garamond Garamond, or Baskerville Baskerville. With historical types it depends on which original design served as the model for the modern type designer. Giambattista Bodoni, for instance, designed a large number of typefaces that might serve as models: they resemble each other, but also vary in many details, and in their gradations of weight. Historical typefaces originally adapted for the Monotype composing system, such as Bembo [see also 9] have sometimes suffered ugly changes in the process of conversion for photo- and crt-composition and for digital form.

a: The original, 24 pt metal Monotype Bembo. b: With greater x-height and reduced extenders, Monotype's 24 pt digitized version appears larger. Something of the original's elegance has been lost. c: A pirated version, also 24 pt, from Compugraphic (the company no longer exists). No further comments needed. For copyright reasons, it was called Bem. Cheap typefaces that come free with PCs are often of this quality.

century to the present day, it was increasingly used mainly for emphasis. As such, it remains the most elegant and yet clearest option for emphasizing individual words or whole pieces of text, whether simply on account of its structural difference with the text type, or, in addition, because of its differing tonal value. (For other emphasis options, see 'Emphasis', p. 44.)

Not till the nineteenth century did 'false' italics occur, under the influence of drawn lithographic lettering. Of all the characteristics of true italics, they have preserved only the secondary characteristic of the slope, but not their fundamental structure [21, 22].

Today, it is possible to 'italicize' a type; that is, to electronically slope an existing roman type. The results are unsatisfactory, as there is no way of taking account of optical considerations. If a typeface lacks an italic, and there is really no alternative to 'italicizing' the roman, the slope should not be steeper than 10°, otherwise the distortions will be too great.

19 Cancellaresca corsiva with hardly perceptible slope. Reduced from a papal brief of 1512. (From FRANZ STEFFENS, *Lateinische Paläographie*. Freiburg i.Ü. 1903.)

si esse posset; tu esses unus profecto; qui & meo iu=
dicio, & omnium uix ullam ceteris oratoribus (pace
horum dixerim) laudem reliquisti. Verum si tibi ip-
si nihil deest , quod in forensibus rebus ciuilibusq; uer
setur , quin scias ; neque eam tamen scientiam quam
adiungis oratori , complexus es : uideamus, ne plus ei
tribuas , quàm res, et ueritas ipsa concedat . Hic Cras
sus , Memento , inquit , me non de mea , sed de orato-

20 The italic used in 1559 by Aldus's son, Paulus Manutius, in a small octavo edition of Cicero (*De oratore, de claribus oratoribus, orator*) had also been used by his father. (Reproduced same-size from the original.)

Sample of Bembo Roman
Sample of Bembo Italic

21 The example of Bembo shows very clearly the structural differences between the roman and italic versions of a classic book type.

a Algarve *Algarve*   b Algarve *Algarve*

22 a: Where there are no structural differences, sloped italics differ from roman type only in their slope. Like Linotype Univers 430, shown here, many sanserifs have 'false' italics. This example was drawn like this by the designer; electronically sloped, 'italicized' versions result in unnatural and unsatisfactory forms. b: A sanserif face with a genuine italic: Scala Sans.

The word

Given that an adult reader's eye registers not individual letters but whole words, or parts of them, it is not surprising that words play a particularly important role in the reading process. With an easily readable typeface the individual letters are always designed with regard to their impact as parts of a word. While being clearly differentiated, they must be capable of fitting together as harmoniously as possible into whole words.

Large amounts of text are generally set in lowercase letters, with capitals at the start of sentences and of some individual words. The x-height, ascenders and descenders of our lowercase letters produce characteristic word-forms, which are further differentiated by accents, the dot on the i, the particular height of t, and of course by the varying contours of each individual letter.

Text set entirely in capitals, by contrast, simply produces patterns of more or less long rectangles. Text in capitals is particularly difficult to read and needs a large amount of space [23, 24].

Clearly differentiated design of the ascenders and descenders is therefore an important requirement. It is not achieved only by making them long enough, but also by the character of the design, for example in the serifs.

The hard-to-read texts that we are sometimes confronted with are often the result of inadequate letterspacing. With any printed matter, the printed area interacts with the unprinted area. This applies equally for the individual line, for the individual words and for the individual letters. In the same way that the whole page should have a consistent, even, but not boring grey tonality, both the lines and the words must also have a consistent grey tonality. (As we have already seen, this is a matter that the type designer needs to take into account in designing the individual letters.) Spotty, uneven words, lines and pages result when the space between the letters is wrong – too great, too little or uneven.

The space between letters is a function of their interior spaces, or counters. The smaller the counter, the smaller the space between letters, and vice versa. This applies not only to the roman alphabet, including blackletter and italic, but also for Greek and Cyrillic, and for all written, drawn and typographic letters [25].

THE RESULTS OF LEGIBILITY ANALYSES CAN BE
CONTRADICTORY, BUT ONE THING IS CLEAR:
TEXT SET IN CAPITALS IS HARDER TO READ THAN
TEXT SET IN UPPER- AND LOWERCASE. THIS
MAY NOT BE PARTICULARLY IMPORTANT IN THE
CASE OF INDIVIDUAL WORDS, BUT IT IS FOR LARGE
AMOUNTS OF TEXT. THEN TOO, THERE IS ALSO
A GREAT DIFFERENCE IN THE AMOUNT OF SPACE
a

The results of legibility analyses can be contradictory, but one thing
is clear: text set in capitals is harder to read than text set in upper-
and lowercase. This may not be particularly important in the case of
individual words, but it is for large amounts of text. Then too, there
is also a great difference in the amount of space required by the text.
b

THE RESULTS OF LEGIBILITY ANALYSES CAN BE CONTRADICTORY,
BUT ONE THING IS CLEAR: TEXT SET IN CAPITALS IS HARDER TO
READ THAN TEXT SET IN UPPER- AND LOWERCASE. THIS MAY
NOT BE PARTICULARLY IMPORTANT IN THE CASE OF INDIVIDUAL
WORDS, BUT IT IS FOR LARGE AMOUNTS OF TEXT. THEN TOO,
THERE IS ALSO A GREAT DIFFERENCE IN THE AMOUNT OF SPACE
c

24   Examples a and b require no further comment. If the type size of the text set
in capitals is so reduced that it does not require much more space than the text set in
upper- and lowercase, it becomes really unreadable (c).

tollere **tollere**   tollere tollere

25   Small counters – little space between letters; large counters – much space between
letters.

In the same way that individual letters become proportionally leaner as they increase in size – and also need to do so in digitized typefaces – letterspaces also become proportionally smaller with increasing type size. (The need for narrower or broader 'set', as it is known, is taken into account, more or less successfully, by manufacturers in programming their typefaces.)

Letterspacing that appears lighter than the median lightness of the counters of the letters concerned produces, in lowercase setting, word-images that appear to fall apart; too tight letterspacing produces blotchy, uneven words [26].

Exceptions: certain types – narrow sanserifs and narrow italics – can be difficult to read in small sizes. In such cases a few additional units of letterspacing can improve their readability. The amount of spacing must be selected on a case-by-case basis, depending on the design and size of the typeface [27].

For the lowercase, there is in theory a right spacing for any given size of type. (At least, the variables concerned are within an extremely narrow range.)

Things are somewhat less straightforward with capitals. Here, the starting point is a minimum space, that can be increased more or less, depending on the situation. The minimum space is determined by the lightness of the biggest counters (C, D, G, O, Q): if any of these letters causes a 'hole' to appear in the word, the spacing is too tight [28].

The spacing may, though, be considerably wider. But this requires appropriate surroundings. Widely spaced capitals require a great deal of space around them, and particularly above and below.

If they are to be readable, capitals require not only to be spaced: the spacing must also be even (which also applies, under different circumstances, to the lowercase). The spacing is even when the spaces appear optically equal.

When this matter is discussed in the professional literature and on courses, reference is often made to the concept of equal areas [29].

However, precisely this example makes it immediately clear that – for example – the space between O and L is greater in area than that between R and T. And what about the spaces between L and W, and T and H? Where does the space between letters begin, and where does the space surrounding a letter itself end? Although the areas

set too loose
and too tight

Extremely narrow or narrow sanserif and italic types can be difficult to read in small sizes. In such cases a few additional units of letterspacing can improve their readability. The amount of spacing depends on the design and size of the typeface.

Extremely narrow or narrow sanserif and italic types can be difficult to read in small sizes. In such cases a few additional units of letterspacing can improve their readability. The amount of spacing depends on the design and size of the typeface.

Futura Light Condensed: the lower text is 3-unit letterspaced.

Extremely narrow or narrow sanserif and italic types can be difficult to read in small sizes. In such cases a few additional units of letterspacing can improve their readability. The amount of spacing depends on the design and size of the typeface.

Extremely narrow or narrow sanserif and italic types can be difficult to read in small sizes. In such cases a few additional units of letterspacing can improve their readability. The amount of spacing depends on the design and size of the

Franklin Gothic Condensed: the lower text is 5-unit letterspaced.

Extremely narrow or narrow sanserif and italic types can be difficult to read in small sizes. In such cases a few additional units of letterspacing can improve their readability. The amount of spacing depends on the design and size of the typeface.

Extremely narrow or narrow sanserif and italic types can be difficult to read in small sizes. In such cases a few additional units of letterspacing can improve their readability. The amount of spacing depends on the design and size of the typeface.

Monotype Baskerville Italic: the lower text is 3-unit letterspaced.

between the letters are not equal, the word appears evenly spaced. So this cannot be a matter of spaces of equal area. If, however, we replace the concept of area with that of light, everything becomes much simpler, and we can do without confusing concepts such as 'residual letterspace'.

Light – the brightness of the unprinted surface – flows from above and below into the interior spaces of the letters and the space between

WORDIMAGES
WORDIMAGES

28   Above, uneven, too tight spacing. Below, minimum spacing – any tighter and R
and D, and the spaces between W and O, O and R, M and A would cause 'holes' to
appear. Whether a word is 'correctly' spaced is often a matter of dispute, also among
typographers.

WOOLWORTH

Letter spacing should not be mechanically
equal but must achieve equal optical space.
The letters must be separated
by even and adequate white areas.

29   From JAN TSCHICHOLD, *Treasury of alphabets and lettering.* New York, 1966.

them. The light coming from above is more effective than that coming from below. This means that the n of a sanserif typeface must
be somewhat wider than the u of the same typeface, if both letters are
to appear equally wide. Similarly, the space between I and A must
be smaller than the space between I and V (given that A and V have
the same angle). This phenomenon is not explicable in terms of equal
areas, but it is in terms of the need for equal light [31].

Non-metal-based composition systems have made it possible not
only to increase, but also to reduce the space between letters [26].
While with metal type it was impossible or technically problematic
to reduce the gaps that appear between some capitals and the following lowercase letters, this is no longer a problem. It is done by 'kerning'. So, what is this?

As with metal type, in digitized type each letter also has a standard
width. The letter itself has an additional space left and right, which
are so determined that the letter will fit well in most combinations –
not too close to the previous letter, nor too far away from the next
one. These spaces are known as the sidebearings [32].

27

A TRIBUTE TO JAN TSCHICHOLD
FROM LONDON

JAN TSCHICHOLD was a brilliant typographer, a practical designer of any printed matter, not only of books, but also of the whole
range of graphic work from labels to large cinema posters. He was
also a distinguished teacher and a considerable author and editor,
writing on a great variety of problems, typo- and calli-graphic, as

---

A TRIBUTE TO JAN TSCHICHOLD
FROM LONDON

JAN TSCHICHOLD was a brilliant typographer, a practical designer
of any printed matter, not only of books, but also of the whole
range of graphic work from labels to large cinema posters. He was
also a distinguished teacher and a considerable author and editor,
writing on a great variety of problems, typo- and calli-graphic, as

30   The first example is taken from the catalogue to the Tschichold exhibition in
Zurich (*Jan Tschichold, Typograph und Schriftentwerfer, 1902–1974 – Das Lebenswerk*,
Kunstgewerbemuseum der Stadt Zürich, 1976). The text was set in 10/12 pt Sabon
on a Linotype linecaster. The second example comes from the Scottish catalogue
for the same exhibition (*Jan Tschichold, typographer and type designer, 1902–1974*,
National Library of Scotland, 1982). Also set in 10 pt Sabon (interlinear space 4.5 mm)
on a Berthold ads 3000 photosetter. (Illustrations reduced approx. 10 %.) Neither
composing system is still in use, which is of no relevance for this comparison.

Although the text of the Scottish catalogue was composed without using 'tracking',
that is, with 'normal' letterspacing, the letters are too tightly spaced (see, e.g., the
sequence illi in brilliant). With almost identical interlinear spacing, the type is too
large, which makes it harder to follow the lines. For these reasons, the text is less inviting than the version above. This has nothing to do with photosetting as such; rather
it is the result of the hyphenation and justification values being chosen carelessly,
according to prevailing fashion.

That the overall impression of a piece of printed matter always depends on the
typographical details can be seen from the following: in the Scottish version, the drop
initial is too big; the lines in capitals are too tightly set, not optically spaced, and
have too little interlinear space. Although the whole layout and (apparently) the
details too were taken over from the Zurich catalogue, the result is unsatisfactory.
(That the Scottish catalogue is 8 mm shorter but the same width, so that the type area
is quite wrongly placed on the page, is part of the same story.)

IA IV u n

31 The space between I and A is optically the same as that between I and V; the counter of u appears the same size as the counter of n. However, measurement reveals that the space between I and V is greater than the space between I and A, and the counter of n is greater in area than the counter of u. The light that flows into the spaces between and within letters from above is 'brighter', more effective.

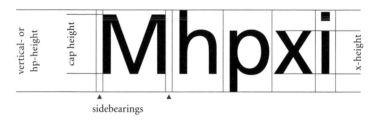

vertical- or hp-height | cap height | x-height

▲ ▲
sidebearings

32 The positioning of a letter in its own space is known as fitting. The starting point for fitting is the em quad, a square with the same width as the vertical or hp height. Each letter or character has its own width, consisting of the character itself plus its sidebearings. For example, in the QuarkXPress page layout program, the em quad is divided into 200 units on the horizontal axis. Depending on the typeface, an M has around 200 units, an i around 50, and a g and h each around 120 units. The more units the quad is divided into, the more even the composition will appear. In Adobe InDesign, the em quad is divided into 1,000 units.

There are, however, combinations that require more or less space than is provided by the standard setting. For such cases, if the typeface is intended for setting continuous text, manufacturers develop kerning tables.

Kerning tables contain those letter combinations for which the standard spacings are altered. The space is usually reduced for such combinations as

Av Ay 'A L' Ta Ty Ve Va Wo Ya Ye

and increased for combinations like

f) f! [f gg gy gf qj

Manufacturers' settings should not be trusted blindly. We still encounter inadequate spacing between capitals and the subsequent

Table Table Table
Verse Verse Verse
Warn Warn Warn
Ypres Ypres Ypres

33   not kerned   too tight   right

fi fè fä fi fè fä *fè fl fk* *fè fl fk*
not kerned kerned not kerned kerned

allfällig allfällig allfällig
f and ä touch f and ä do not touch f and ä touch;
but doesn't this
look better than
34   the middle version?

find flying effective efficient shuffle
find flying effective efficient shuffle
find flying effective efficient shuffle
find flying effective efficient shuffle

35   Standard roman and italic ligatures, compared with the individual letters.

lowercase letters. This is a survival from the early days of non-metal composition when, in the sheer euphoria of being able to justify more tightly, much photosetting was far too tightly spaced. Capitals have bigger counters than their lowercase, and require an appropriate amount of space [33].

Many typefaces, and particularly italics, also need additional kerning for the lowercase. Generally speaking, individual letters should not touch. A small 'hole' between two letters is less bad than letters that collide with each other. But here too, there may be exceptions – decisions require common sense and a trained eye [34].

It is possible to correct an existing kerning table, or to supplement it with additional combinations, but care is needed: the corrections should not be perceptible, nor should they create any collisions with floating accents. A serious set of kerning values can only apply to a single language, for each language has its own critical letter combinations.

Another aspect of the word is ligatures. These are generally composed of two or three joined-together letters. Standard ligatures include fi, fl, ff, ffi and ffl [35].

The line

The line is the third unit of detail typography, after the letter and the word. Wordspaces, the spaces before and after punctuation, as well as line length, are important matters for typographers. While all the issues that concern letters and words apply for all forms of continuous text, considerations about the line must also take account of the nature of the piece of typography in question.

This applies particularly to the length of the line, or measure, as it is also known. An academic work, which needs to include wide mathematical formulas, table or diagrams, will, unless double-column setting is an option, naturally have longer lines than a novel, a reference work, a leisure magazine for entertainment, or a daily paper. Lines that are either too short or too long are tiring, and thus detract from readability.

This is not a real problem with the often (too) short lines of reference works, in that they seldom require the reading of large amounts of text. Typographers recommend an optimum of between 50 and 60 or between 60 and 70 characters per line. Tinker claims that a 10 pt type with 2 pt interlinear spacing is equally readable at measures between 14 and 31 picas (about 6 to 13 cm), but also notes that 'reader preferences quite definitely favor moderate line widths. Relatively long and very short line widths are disliked. In general, printing practice seems to be adjusted to the desires of the average reader with regard to line width.'

It appears that, here too, there is a remarkable discrepancy between optical legibility and being inviting to read (see p. 54 below).

The relative legibility of a line depends not only on its length, but also on the right wordspacing and the type of composition.

There is no question but that wordspaces may not be too large, or that the line must appear to be an even, well-balanced whole. What applies to letterspaces also applies to wordspaces: they too are a function of the counters of the individual letters: the smaller these are, the smaller the wordspaces; the larger the counters, the larger the wordspaces [36].

The generally applicable rule for wordspacing is: as much as necessary, as little as possible. A clear but not excessive space will normally be around a quarter of the notional body size, e.g. 2.5 points

as compared with the contents of its wine-
cellars ? What position would its expenditure on literature take, as compared with its
expenditure on luxurious eating ? We talk
of food for the mind, as of food for the
body : now a good book contains such food
inexhaustibly ; it is a provision for life, and

37 To be able to set as much type as possible in as little time as possible – most
compositors were paid piece rates – in the nineteenth and early twentieth centuries
lines were often justified with en spaces, i.e. the spaces between the word were half
the body size of the type in question. (Example from JOHN RUSKIN, *Sesame and lilies*,
Orpington: George Allen, 1887.)

This line is too loosely wordspaced.
This line is too tightly wordspaced.
This line is correctly wordspaced.

38 In cases of uncertainty too tight wordspacing is preferable to too loose wordspacing.

a These lines are set in the same type

b These lines are set in the same

c These lines are set in the same t

39 Lines a and b are set in the same typeface, with the same wordspacing; the
spacing appears too loose in the larger size. If it is slightly reduced, the line appears
more attractive (c).

for 10 pt type. But here too, ultimately, the critical eye must decide [37, 38]. Smaller sizes of type require proportionally more space, and larger sizes proportionally less [39].

Justified composition is typesetting in which all the lines are spaced to be of equal length. The space that would otherwise be left over at the end of the line is distributed between the words: this is known as justifying the lines. If there is a good deal of space left over at the end of the line, the wordspaces in the line can be reduced to get another word, or at least another syllable, into the line. If this is not possible, it becomes necessary to increase the wordspacing until the line is filled out ('driving it out' is the trade expression). If the measure is wide enough, neither of these operations should be noticeable; good justified composition has an even, neutral appearance. For English composition, a line length of between 60 and 70 characters (as in this book) represents a reasonable compromise between the optimum number of characters in the line and evenly-spaced composition. Other values apply for other languages: words are longer in German than in English, French or Italian, for example, so German may require longer lines.

If the measure is too narrow – with less than around 50 characters per line – even wordspacing becomes difficult, if not impossible. The wordspaces become obviously uneven and large 'holes' appear. These problems can be avoided with unjustified or 'ragged' setting, where the wordspaces are all the same, and the right-hand end of the line varies in length.

Unjustified setting is not restricted to narrow measures, but can also be used for measures that would be suited for justified setting. In such cases, it will be selected for aesthetic, design considerations: the even wordspacing within the lines makes the text appear more regular, but at the same time, the irregular right-hand margin makes it appear more lively.

Unjustified setting can be produced in two ways:
1. Unjustified setting with no word breaks and no further attention [40a]. Depending on the nature of the work, this rather crude, unpolished form may be entirely appropriate.
2. Unjustified setting with reasonable word breaks and an appropriate 'hyphenation zone' (the distance between the longest and the

What is good typography? An elegant book page, designed in accordance with traditional principles, or an amusingly designed avant-garde page? Any rapid decision in favour of one or the other solution reveals more about a person's approach to aesthetics than it does about the quality of the typography. So, the question should be: What job does the book have to do?

a

What is good typography? An elegant book page, designed in accordance with traditional principles, or an amusingly designed avant-garde page? Any rapid decision in favour of one or the other solution reveals more about a person's approach to aesthetics than it does about the quality of the typography. So, the question should be: What job does the book have to do?

b

40

shortest lines). This generally has about the same number of characters in the line, or not many fewer, as justified setting.

The 'hyphenation zone' should not be too wide. Wherever possible, irregular rhythms, 'staircases', 'holes' and single words standing at the end of lines should be avoided [40a], as should bad word breaks. Unjustified setting with a wide hyphenation zone (with a 'hard rag') looks uneven and unsettled, even if the rhythm of the long and short lines is regular; then, it looks more like poetry than it is entitled to. In unjustified setting with a narrow hyphenation zone, the text is given a 'soft rag' [40b].

35

Perfect unjustified setting is very demanding and difficult to achieve, and is thus rarely encountered.

Many rules concerning the space before or after certain capital letters or punctuation marks that were once observed as a matter of course in good typography are widely ignored today. They are, however, important not only for the even appearance of the composition, but also for the easy understanding of the text. Depending on the typeface, the appropriate units must be added or subtracted. Thus : ; ? ! and ' should be separated from the final letter of the preceding word by a clear space. Similarly, brackets, quotation marks, superior figures and asterisks should not stand too close to the preceding or following letters. If the type manufacturer has not taken account of this in the kerning program, manual intervention will be required in such cases [41].

In the same way that the wordspaces must be somewhat reduced after letters with too much 'body' (A T V W and Y), they must also be reduced after abbreviation points (fig. Prof. no. etc.) [42].

An unfortunate usage that is often encountered is too little space between the initials of forenames, followed by excessive space between the initials and the surname [43]. And correct use should be made of all the other punctuation marks; they are not as unimportant as their insignificant appearance might suggest [44, 45].

The ellipsis (…) is a sign of its own. It indicates omissions, and can be replaced by three full points (...). If this is done, they must be spaced. Which option is used will depend on the typeface in question [46].

Dashes are often used incorrectly. There is a distinction between the hyphen (-) and the dash, which can also be a minus sign. This is either the em dash (—), which extends over the whole width of the notional body of type, or the so-called en dash (–), which is actually seldom exactly half the body width. The hyphen should not be used for functions for which a dash is reserved [47–50].

The diagonal solidus stroke (/) is often set without space between two words, which can result in nonsensical situations [51].

If measurements are given in running text, the multiplication sign (×), while correct in itself, is too obtrusive, and should accordingly be replaced by the x of the typeface being used [52]. Both British and American usage has traditionally favoured double quotation marks

Typography:	Typography:	'I feel'	'I feel'
Typography;	Typography;	"I feel"	"I feel"
Typography?	Typography?	›I feel‹	›I feel‹
Typography!	Typography!	»I feel«	»I feel«
T'graphy	T'graphy	‹I feel›	‹I feel›
Typography²	Typography²	«I feel»	«I feel»
Typography*	Typography*	(I feel)	(I feel)
too close	correctly spaced	[I feel]	[I feel]
41		too close	correctly spaced

Prof. Dr. Peter Weber e. g. 5. 6. 2005
Prof. Dr. Peter Weber e. g. 5.6.2005

42 Wordspaces after abbreviation points generally appear too large (upper line); reduced spaces keep the words better grouped.

The exhibition featured paintings by the Romantic artist C.E.F.H. Blechen and by K.R.H. Sonderborg.

The exhibition featured paintings by the Romantic artist C. E. F. H. Blechen and by K. R. H. Sonderborg.

43 Forename initials should not be set too close to each other or be optically separated from the surname, as in the upper example.

Set the word you want to emphasize in *italic;* that will make it stand out.
Set the word you want to emphasize in *italic*; that will make it stand out.

44 Purely visually, colons, semi-colons and other punctuation marks that follow a word or phrase set in italic look better set in italic than in roman. This is however not logical, as the punctuation marks are part of the sentence as a whole.

1:2 2:3 3:4   1 : 2 2 : 3 3 : 4   1:2 2:3 3:4

45 Colons between figures appear too close if they are unspaced; normal wordspacing produces 'holes'. The third group shows them correctly spaced; the spacing needs to be consistent with the overall typography.

well, I'll be bl…! (…) […]

a b

'…' "…" Mr … had already been in …

c d

46   If parts of words are omitted, the ellipsis should follow the last letter with no extra space, nor should there be any space before the punctuation (a). It should also not have spaces on either side within parentheses and quotation marks (b, c). If it replaces omitted words, however, the ellipsis should have wordspaces on either side (d). If it occurs at the end of a sentence, there should be no full point, though a question mark or exclamation mark should be used if necessary (a). In the case of (a), (b) and (c) attention must be paid to the kerning; spaces may need to be increased or reduced.

semi-precious   Cobden-Sanderson   two- or three-dimensional

47   The hyphen (-) is used at the end of the line to divide broken words, or to link two words, or to link connected parts of a phrase.

Here – look!   'Push off, or I'll – !'   'You sad –!'
He came – the very same day – but he had changed.

48   The en dash is used to link phrases or indicate omissions, or with an inserted clause. In some English practices – notably that of Oxford University Press – and especially in American-English style, an em dash (without space before and after) is prescribed.

Clacton-on-Sea–London   London–Glasgow
18.15–20.30

49   The en dash is used to indicate spans of distance or time. In neither case should the dash collide with the adjacent letters or figures. The minimal spaces should appear equal on both sides – which also applies to hyphens.

for quotations, with single quotation marks being used for quotations within quotations. A more attractive appearance is achieved by using single quotation marks for the more frequently occurring quotations, and the double version for the less frequent occurrence of quotations within quotations [53]. By the way, the 'guillemets' used

The typefaces used
– Adobe Minion Regular
– Adobe Minion Expert Regular
– Adobe Minion Italic
– Futura Bold

a

The typefaces used
– Adobe Minion Regular
– Adobe Minion Expert Regular
– Adobe Minion Italic
– Futura Bold

b

The typefaces used
• Adobe Minion Regular
• Adobe Minion Expert Regular
• Adobe Minion Italic
• Futura Bold

c

The typefaces used
· Adobe Minion Regular
· Adobe Minion Expert Regular
· Adobe Minion Italic
· Futura Bold

d

50   The en dash used for lists. It is separated from the following word by one or more wordspaces. The dash can be replaced by either bold (c) or normal (d) centred points. The style chosen will depend on the typeface and the text; depending on the typographic design, the points or dashes may be aligned under the line above (a, c) or hung out (b, d).

Pablo Casals/Alfred Cortot/Jacques Thibaud
Pablo Casals / Alfred Cortot / Jacques Thibaud

51   A piece of typographical nonsense often encountered: solidus strokes set un-spaced – that which belongs together has been pulled apart.

in some European languages to indicate quotations (« ») are set with the points facing outwards, as shown here, in France and Switzerland, but with the points facing inwards in Germany.

Abbreviations in capitals are often too obtrusive, and interfere with the smooth flow of the line. Instead of capitals, they can be set in small caps, but this may look strange. Another possibility – and often the best – is to set the abbreviation a half or one size smaller, depending on the typeface. The weight of the letters will no longer be identical with that of the continuous text, but this is optically hardly noticeable [54]. (See also the discussion of capitals under 'Emphasis', p. 44.)

39

Two of Marc's pictures measured 150 × 105 cm, and one
was 70 × 56 cm. His other works were small;
the smallest, a water-colour, no more than 10 × 12 cm.

Two of Marc's pictures measured 150 x 105 cm, and one
was 70 x 56 cm. His other works were small;
the smallest, a water-colour, no more than 10 x 12 cm.

52   Although it is the only correct usage in mathematical texts, in non-mathematical
texts the multiplication sign (×) is too obtrusive, and should be replaced by the x
of the typeface used, which will invariably be recognized as a multiplication sign.
The spaces either side of the x look better when, as here, they are slightly less than
a wordspace.

Typography involves "the selection of the right typeface, readability,
order, the logical positioning of the components", as well as "a meti-
culous attention to detail" – a reminder of "an oft-quoted remark
by Rodin: 'It's the detail that makes a masterpiece.'" Similarly, Max
Caflisch believes that it is not merely "erroneous, indeed absurd" to
think that typography must

Typography involves 'the selection of the right typeface, readability,
order, the logical positioning of the components', as well as 'a meti-
culous attention to detail' – a reminder of 'an oft-quoted remark
by Rodin: "It's the detail that makes a masterpiece."' Similarly, Max
Caflisch believes that it is not merely 'erroneous, indeed absurd' to
think that typography must

53   Above: customary usage. Below: the appearance is improved by using the
more obtrusive double quotation marks for the less frequent quotations within
quotations.

At BBC headquarters in London
At ʙʙᴄ headquarters in London
At BBC headquarters in London

54   (a) Capitals the same size as the text type. (b) Small caps the same size as the
text type. (c) Capitals 1 pt smaller than the text type.

Numerals

Seven is a number, but 7 is a numeral. The terms 'number' and 'numeral' are often confused. A number stands for a quantitative concept; a numeral is a graphic sign that represents a number. As numerals are usually part of any more complex text setting, they are dealt with in this chapter. They are referred to here, as is normal in typography, as 'figures'.

Western civilization is familiar with the Roman numerals, represented by letters (I V X L C D M), and the arabic numerals 0 to 9.

With arabic numerals, there are lining figures, non-lining figures, and also small cap figures, superiors and inferiors, and fractions.

Lining figures are all the same height: usually the same as the capitals or slightly less. They are normally set on a constant (en) body, so they can be used as tabular figures. Non-lining figures, by contrast, have individual widths. Increasingly typefaces are being provided with individual and constant widths for either, or indeed both, the lining or the non-lining figures [55].

Small cap figures, i.e. figures with the same height as the small caps, are rarely found. If available, they should be used; if not, non-lining figures should be used with small caps [56].

To prevent large numbers becoming difficult to read, the numerals are grouped in threes, separated by commas, starting from the back. In scientific publications, the commas may be replaced with spaces [57].

Superior figures should be separated from the preceding letter by a small but unmistakable space [see also 41]. The same applies to inferior figures, which should lie somewhat below the line. Both lining and non-lining figures are suitable for use as superiors and inferiors, depending on the typeface used. As they are sometimes too small, or too large, or are not correctly placed with regard to the baseline, it may be necessary to change the default settings to arrive at a satisfactory result [58].

Both the lining and the non-lining figure 1 are often placed on a too wide body, as in the Minion typeface used in this book, which results in undesirable spaces, and from time to time requires manual correction [59].

a 0 1 2 3 4 5 6 7 8 9

b 0 1 2 3 4 5 6 7 8 9

c 0 1 2 3 4 5 6 7 8 9

1214960	4128154	2524901
4031257	3102476	1816382
a	b	c

55 Trinité 2: lining figures (a) and non-lining figures (b) for tables, both with the same, 1-en width; non-lining figures with individual widths (c), unsuitable for tabular work, but appropriate for running text [see 61].

0123456789 SMALL CAPS
WITH SMALL CAP FIGURES

0123456789 SMALL CAPS
WITH NON-LINING FIGURES

56 A few typefaces (such Linotype Syntax, shown here) have small cap figures (a). If they are not available, non-lining figures may be used with small caps (b).

| 4,719 | 46,865 | 396,781 | 23,546,719 |
| 4 719 | 46 865 | 396 781 | 23 546 719 |

57

a mathematical symbol[16] H_2O Pb_3O_4

58 Minion has specially designed superior and inferior figures, with uniform width like the lining figures, but with significantly broader proportions than the lining figures.

a Lining figure 1.   b Lining figure 1.

59 Uncorrected spaces before and after the lining figure 1 (a); the same situation with manual corrections (b).

a   ½ ¾ ⅞ fractions
b   ½ ¾ ⅞ fractions
c $^1/_2$ $^3/_4$ $^7/_8$ fractions

60   Specially designed fractions look best: their weight matches the typeface being used – Minion, in this case (a). Example b shows fractions assembled from superior and inferior non-lining figures and special fraction diagonals, which appear too weak. Fractions assembled out of superior and inferior lining figures and the standard solidus stroke are entirely unsatisfactory (c).

In 1329 Albrecht V von Hohenberg returned to Constance from his stay in Paris. In 1307 two Konrad Blarers appear as witnesses. Which of them is referred to in the subsequent documents from 1299 to 1316 is uncertain. At all events, there is no Konrad recorded as mayor up to 1316. There is, however, a Konrad Blarer mentioned among the councillors in 1319, and

In 1329 Albrecht V von Hohenberg returned to Constance from his stay in Paris. In 1307 two Konrad Blarers appear as witnesses. Which of them is referred to in the subsequent documents from 1299 to 1316 is uncertain. At all events, there is no Konrad recorded as mayor up to 1316. There is, however, a Konrad Blarer mentioned among the councillors in 1319, and

61   The same text, with lining figures (above) and non-lining figures (below). The excessive spacing of the lining figure 1 in the upper example has not been corrected [see also 59].

Fractions can be set with lining or non-lining figures: here too, the decision should be based on the typeface used, or the specific typographical situation. Some typefaces have special fraction figures. They are already correctly positioned, are stronger, as they have not been reduced in size, and thus fit much better into the overall composition. Their diagonals are also somewhat more acutely angled than the ordinary solidus stroke, which should not be used in their place [60].

As with words in capitals, lining figures are over-obtrusive in running text, and create a restless appearance. They should be restricted to tabular work, and non-lining figures used wherever possible in continuous text. Lining figures are also often not ideally justified, and require additional kerning or individual attention [61].

Many sanserifs have only lining figures. And there are a very few typefaces, such as Monotype Bell or Microsoft Georgia, that do not distinguish between lining and non-lining figures. Their 'standard figures' are so designed that they are only a little taller than the x-height, and thus do not disturb the flow of the text.

Emphasis

The classic means of giving emphasis to a word or phrase in continuous text is to set it in italic. Common experience suggests that italic is somewhat slower to read than roman type, and its use in large quantities is not appreciated by readers. Used sparingly, it has the advantage of attracting the reader's attention without disturbing the flow of the text.

The same is true of small caps. These are capitals whose optical height is the same as the x-height of the lowercase. They cannot be substituted by a smaller size of capitals, as these will look too pale, on account of their reduction in size. The weight of true small caps is the same as that of their uppercase and lowercase, but their proportions are broader than those of the capitals [62–64]. Whether or not small caps should be spaced is sometimes disputed; in the author's opinion, this will depend on the design of the type. At all events, readability is generally noticeably improved when small caps are slightly, and more or less evenly spaced. When text is set in small caps, words that begin with a capital letter need also here to begin with a full capital.

Other forms of emphasis – text set in capitals, the semi-bold or bold versions of the text type, underlining, a larger size of type, a different typeface, the use of a second colour or tones – produce a restless effect, and hinder linear reading. Such forms of emphasis can, however, be not only appropriate but necessary in reference works and schoolbooks, and also have a refreshing effect in experimental books.

a CAPITALS   SMALL CAPITALS

b CAPITALS   SMALL CAPITALS

c CAPITALS   SMALL CAPITALS

62   Capitals and their small caps. a: 15 pt Lexicon 2 Roman A; b: 16 pt Scala Sans Regular; c: 16 pt Minion Regular; capitals evenly spaced at 17 units, small caps at 12 units, but not optically balanced.

a CAPITALS AND SMALL CAPITALS

b CAPITALS AND SMALL CAPITALS

c CAPITALS AND SMALL CAPITALS

d CAPITALS AND SMALL CAPITALS

63   a: 11 pt Minion Regular capitals; b: 16 pt Minion small caps, set to the same height as a, to compare the proportions.
c: 11 pt Scala Sans Regular capitals; d: 15 pt Scala Sans Regular small caps, set to the same height as c, to compare the proportions.

The following style makes it easiest to identify entries in a bibliography: author's surname and forename in CAPITALS and SMALL CAPITALS, the book title in *italics*, all other information in roman; the second and subsequent lines indented one em. Articles in books, newspapers and journals in quotation marks.

The following style makes it easiest to identify entries in a bibliography: author's surname and forename in CAPITALS und SMALL CAPITALS, the book title in *italics*, all other information in roman; the second and subsequent lines indented one em. Articles in books, newspapers and journals in quotation marks.

64   Above: set with false small caps (smaller-sized capitals). Below: the same text with true small caps, whose weight matches that of the text type. They are here slightly, and more or less evenly spaced.

who receives a stipend as an officer of the Royal Household, writes court-odes, etc. The first recorded appointment by authority to the office of Poet Laureate was a 'warrant for a grant' to Dryden, on 13 April, 1668; confirmed by patent of 18 Aug., 1670. **3.** Langage l. LYDGATE. The laureat strain of Pindar GROTE. **B.** *sb.* **1.** = *Poet laureate* 1529. **b.** A court panegyrist 1863. **2.** *U.S.* A degree title awarded in some institutions to women. BRYCE. **3.** *Numism.* = LAUREL *sb.* 4. 1727. **1.** The courtly laureat pays His quit-rent ode, his pepper corn of praise COWPER. Hence **Lau·reate-ship.**

Laureate (lǫ·ri₁e¹t), *v. Obs. exc. Hist.* ME. [In sense 1 – med.L. *laureare* (see prec.); in sense 2 f. LAUREATE A 2.] **1.** *trans.* To crown with laurel as victor, poet, or the like; to confer honourable distinction upon. **2.** *spec.* **a.** To graduate or confer a University degree upon. **b.** To appoint (a poet) to the office of Laureate. 1637.
1. By his reygne is all Englonde lawreat 1509.

Laureation (lǫri₁e¹·ʃən). 1637. [– med.L. *laureatio* (XIII), f. *laureare* crown with laurels, f. L. *laureus* LAUREL *sb.*; see -ATION.] The action of crowning with laurel or making laureate; in the Sc. Universities, a term for graduation or admission to a degree; also, the creation of a poet laureate.

Laurel (lǫ·rēl), *sb.* ME. (**lorer, laurer,** later, **lorel,** etc.) [– OFr. *lorier* (mod. *laurier*) – Pr. *laurier,* f. *laur* (= OFr. *lor,* Cat. *llor,* etc.) :– L. *laurus,* prob. of Mediterranean origin. The later form is due to dissimilation of *r . . r* to *r . . l*; cf. Sp. *laurel.*] **1.** The Bay-tree or Bay-laurel, *Laurus nobilis*; see BAY *sb.¹* **2.** Now *rare,* exc. as in 2. **b.** Any plant of the genus *Laurus* or the N.O. *Lauraceæ.* LINDLEY. **2.** The foliage of this tree as an emblem of victory or of distinction in poetry, etc. **a.** *collect. sing.* ME. **b.** *pl.* 1585. **c.** A branch or wreath of this tree (*lit.* and *fig.*) ME. **†d.** The dignity of Poet Laureate –1814. **3.** In mod. use, applied to *Cerasus laurocerasus* and other trees having

Chem. A crystalline substance ($C_{22}H_{30}O_3$) obtained from the berries of *Laurus nobilis.*

Laurite (lǫ·rəit). 1866. [Named by Wöhler, 1866, after Mrs. *Laura* Joy; see -ITE¹ 2 b.] *Min.* Sulphide of ruthenium, found with platinum in small brilliant crystals.

Laurustine (lǫ·rŏstəin). Also *erron.* **†lauri-, laure-.** 1683. [Englished form of next.] = next.

Laurustinus (lǫ:rŏstəi·nŏs). 1664. [– mod. L. *laurus tinus,* i.e. *laurus* laurel, *tinus* wild laurel.] An evergreen winter-flowering shrub, *Viburnum tinus.*

Laus(e, obs. ff. LOOSE *a.*

†Lauti·tious, *a.* [f. L. *lautitia* magnificence (f. *lautus* washed, sumptuous) + -OUS.] Sumptuous. HERRICK.

Lauwine (lǫ·win, G. lauvī·nə). Also **law-.** 1818. [– G. *lawine,* †*lauwin(e,* etc., of Swiss origin. Ult. origin unknown.] An avalanche.

Lava (lã·vă). 1750. [– It. *lava* †stream suddenly caused by rain, applied in Neapolitan dial. to a lava-stream from Vesuvius, f. *lavare* LAVE *v.¹*] **†1.** A stream of molten rock issuing from the crater of a volcano or from fissures in the earth. **2.** The fluid or semi-fluid matter flowing from a volcano 1760. Also *fig.* **3.** The substance that results from the cooling of the molten rock 1750. **b.** A kind of lava, a bed of lava 1796. **4.** *attrib.* 1802.
Comb.: **l.-millstone,** a hard and coarse basaltic millstone, obtained from quarries near Andernach on the Rhine; **-ware,** a kind of stoneware, manufactured and coloured to assume the semi-vitreous appearance of l.

‖Lavabo (lăvē¹·bo). 1740. [L., = 'I will wash'.] **1.** *Eccl.* **a.** The ritual washing of the celebrant's hands at the offertory, accompanied by the saying of Ps. 25[6]:6–12, beginning *Lavabo inter innocentes manus meas.* **b.** The small towel, also the basin, used in this rite. **2.** A washing-trough used in some mediæval monasteries 1883.

---

65 Lexicons, dictionaries, and other reference works are hardly ever read in a linear fashion. But in encyclopaedias and large, multi-volume reference works entries for a particular keyword often stretch over several columns or even pages, and the detail typography of the text type requires careful attention. This dictionary suggests the kind of articulation of the text that may be needed: bold, italics, small caps, and certain punctuation marks are all used for a distinct purpose. A job like this is a challenge for any typographer. Example reduced by 87%, from *The shorter Oxford English dictionary* (3rd edn, Oxford, 1973).

46

Linespacing, the column

The readability of a text is influenced not only by the choice of typeface, type size, correct or incorrect letter- and wordspacing, and the length of line, but also by the linespacing or interlinear space, often termed 'leading'. Tinker points to the interdependence of line-spacing, type size, and length of line, and emphasizes the great influence that the space between the lines has on readability.

The longer the line, the more linespacing it needs, for a given typeface and type size. Equally, lighter typefaces – generally those with large counters – need more linespacing than darker ones. The internal form of the letters thus influences not only the letter- and wordspacing, but also the linespacing. For typographers, the linespacing is an important means for changing the 'colour', the grey tone of a piece of composition [66].

A question that arises in connection with justified text is that of 'optical margin alignment'. This is less important with smaller type sizes than with larger sizes, but should be applied whenever technically possible; the composition appears quieter, even in small sizes [67].

There is an old compositor's rule that there should never be more than three successive word-breaks under each other at the ends of lines. But if the only way to obey this rule were to remake the page with large gaps in one or more lines, this would be worse for both the appearance and the readability of the text than four or even five successive word-breaks.

Vertical 'rivers' of white space occur on a page when the word-spaces in several lines fall exactly, or almost exactly, under one another. As they disturb the flow of the text, the page make-up should be adjusted to avoid them.

It may be asked whether this is the place to deal with the matter of indenting the first line of a paragraph, or whether this rather belongs to considerations about the layout, which do not concern us here. As Tschichold repeatedly and convincingly stipulated, indenting is essential to the comfortable reading of long texts, and so it is mentioned here. The use of line spaces to separate paragraphs breaks up the page, requires too much space, and creates problems when a paragraph ends at the bottom of a page. In every case, indents are the only certain indicators of a new paragraph [68].

Typography may be defined as the art of rightly disposing printing material in accordance with specific purpose; of so arranging the letters, distributing the space and controlling the type as to aid to the maximum the reader's comprehension of the text. Typography is the efficient means to an esentially utilitarian and only accidentally aesthetic end, for enjoyment of patterns is rarely the reader's chief aim. Therefore, any disposition of printing material which, whatever the intention, has the effect of coming between author and reader is wrong. Stanley Morison

Typography may be defined as the art of rightly disposing printing material in accordance with specific purpose; of so arranging the letters, distributing the space and controlling the type as to aid to the maximum the reader's comprehension of the text. Typography is the efficient means to an esentially utilitarian and only accidentally aesthetic end, for enjoyment of patterns is rarely the reader's chief aim. Therefore, any disposition of printing material which, whatever the intention, has the effect of coming between author and reader is wrong. *Stanley Morison*

Typography may be defined as the art of rightly disposing printing material in accordance with specific purpose; of so arranging the letters, distributing the space and controlling the type as to aid to the maximum the reader's comprehension of the text. Typography is the efficient means to an esentially utilitarian and only accidentally aesthetic end, for enjoyment of patterns is rarely the reader's chief aim. Therefore, any disposition of printing material which, whatever the intention, has the effect of coming between author and reader is wrong.   Stanley Morison

Typography may be defined as the art of rightly disposing printing material in accordance with specific purpose; of so arranging the letters, distributing the space and controlling the type as to aid to the maximum the reader's comprehension of the text. Typography is the efficient means to an esentially utilitarian and only accidentally aesthetic end, for enjoyment of patterns is rarely the reader's chief aim. Therefore, any disposition of printing material which, whatever the intention, has the effect of coming between author and reader is wrong.   *Stanley Morison*

Typography may be defined as the art of rightly disposing printing material in accordance with specific purpose; of so arranging the letters, distributing the space and controlling the type as to aid to the maximum the reader's comprehension of the text. Typography is the efficient means to an esentially utilitarian and only accidentally aesthetic end, for enjoyment of patterns is rarely the reader's chief aim. Therefore, any disposition of printing material which, whatever the intention, has the effect of coming between author and reader is wrong.   STANLEY MORISON

TYPOGRAPHY may be defined as the art of rightly disposing printing material in accordance with specific purpose; of so arranging the letters, distributing the space and controlling the type as to aid to the maximum the reader's comprehension of the text. Typography is the efficient means to an esentially utilitarian and only accidentally aesthetic end, for enjoyment of patterns is rarely the reader's chief aim. Therefore, any disposition of printing material which, whatever the intention, has the effect of coming between author and reader is wrong.

STANLEY MORISON

66   Six versions of the same text, set with the same size of the same type. The versions still look different: the overall impression is affected by both the linespacing and the general arrangement of the text. From top to bottom and left to right: 10 pt Minion Regular set with 0, 1, 2, 3, 4 and 6 pt leading (interlinear space).

In order to enhance both the attractiveness and the readability of a text, it is sometimes necessary to reduce the size of the type while keeping the same linespacing. The optically greater linespacing thus produced makes it easier to follow the lines [69].

If a page includes passages of text in a smaller size of type, with less interlinear space, the main text that follows must resume the main baseline grid. Whether or not such inserts are indented will depend

49

Typography is not an art. Typography
is not a science. Typography is a craft.
Not a craft in the sense of blindly following some poorly understood rules,
a but rather in the sense of the precise

Typography is not an art. Typography
is not a science. Typography is a craft.
Not a craft in the sense of blindly following some poorly understood rules,
b but rather in the sense of the precise

Typography is not an art. Typography is not a science. Typography
is a craft. A craft not in the sense of blindly following some poorly understood rules, but rather in the sense of the precise application of
tried and tested experience. The typographer must know how the
book will be read, what purpose it serves, in order to develop its concept. The typographer is as little responsible for the content of the
book as is the interior designer for the thoughts of the person who
sits on the chair he designed. The chair must be comfortable and suf-
c ficiently robust – no more than that.

Typography is not an art. Typography is not a science. Typography
is a craft. A craft not in the sense of blindly following some poorly understood rules, but rather in the sense of the precise application of
tried and tested experience. The typographer must know how the
book will be read, what purpose it serves, in order to develop its concept. The typographer is as little responsible for the content of the
book as is the interior designer for the thoughts of the person who
sits on the chair he designed. The chair must be comfortable and suf-
d ficiently robust – no more than that.

67   From above around 12 pt, the right-hand margin looks considerably more even
with margin alignment (b), but the appearance of smaller sizes is also improved by
automated alignment (d).

Gutenberg can no longer be our paradigm. Gutenberg can no longer tell us what we should do, but only make us quietly aware of what we should not do: What we should not do is copy handwritten patterns when designing type. Even as a concept this is wrong, and it invariably produces dubious results, which

a always look artificial, if not downright kitsch

Gutenberg can no longer be our paradigm. Gutenberg can no longer tell us what we should do, but only make us quietly aware of what we should not do: What we should not do is copy handwritten patterns when designing type. Even as a concept this is wrong, and it invariably produces dubious results,

b which always look artificial, if not downright kitsch

Gutenberg can no longer be our paradigm. Gutenberg can no longer tell us what we should do, but only make us quietly aware of what we should not do: What we should not do is copy handwritten patterns when designing type. Even as a concept this is wrong, and it invariably produces dubious results, which

c always look artificial, if not downright kitsch

Gutenberg can no longer be our paradigm. Gutenberg can no longer tell us what we should do, but only make us quietly aware of what we should not do: What we should not do is copy handwritten patterns when designing type. Even as a concept this is wrong, and it invariably produces dubious results,

d which always look artificial, if not downright kitsch

68   Whether the text is justified (a, b) or not (c, d), indents alone clearly indicate where a new paragraph begins. All the other theoretically possible way of indicating new paragraphs either need more space (line spaces, lines) or look unfamiliar (paragraph signs, bold or medium centred dots, diagonal slashes, etc. in continuous text).

For me, typography is essentially giving an articulated statement a form appropriate to that statement. The most important element of typographic articulation is white space. There is only 'practical' typography: all other applications of typography are fundament-
a ally free graphic design or some means of psychotherapy or

For me, typography is essentially giving an articulated statement a form appropriate to that statement. The most important element of typographic articulation is white space. There is only 'practical' typography: all other applications of typography are fundamentally free
b graphic design or some means of psychotherapy or

For me, typography is essentially giving an articulated statement a form appropriate to that statement. The most important element of typographic articulation is white space. There is only 'practical' typography: all other applications of typography are fundamentally free
c graphic design or some means of psychotherapy or

For me, typography is essentially giving an articulated statement a form appropriate to that statement. The most important element of typographic articulation is white space. There is only 'practical' typography: all other applications of typography are fundamentally free graphic design or some
d means of psychotherapy or

69   One larger, and one slightly smaller size of type, with the same linespacing. Examples a and b: 10.5/10.5 pt Bembo and 10.0/10.5 pt Bembo. Examples c and d: 9.5/11 pt Scala Sans and 9.0/11 pt Scala Sans. The improved readability of b and d, due to the greater interlinear space, more than compensates for the smaller size of type.

Likewise, if, as post-1688 ideology insisted, monarchs were no longer kings by Divine Right but by contract, on what grounds could fathers and husbands legitimately claim their ascendency over women?

Wife and servant are the same,
But only differ in the name.

In a modest couplet Lady Mary Chudleigh thus got to the heart of the gender, if not the servant, problem!

70   The main text following an inserted passage, in a smaller size and with less interlinear space, must return to the baseline of the basic grid, so that the lines remain in register.

on the overall typographic design. If there is no indent, the typography will appear less disjointed. On the other hand, it may look strange if – as in our example – the lines of the inserted text are very short. Any indent for the inserted passage should match the indent of the main text [70].

In the same way that the design and size of the type, the length of the line, the linespacing, and the style of the setting all determine the overall appearance of the composition, this too – the type area, the sum of all the lines – also has an effect on all the other components of typography, and on the proportions of the margins in particular: in typography, details can never be considered in isolation. However, to move on to consider issues concerning the position of the type area on the page would be to move away from the main focus of this book – detail typography.

The qualities of type

All the well-known and frequently used typefaces are equally legible. And much the same is true of their semi-bold versions; sanserifs too are more or less equally legible. Tinker, who, among others, reached this conclusion, does however mention that his respondents found the sanserif he used (Kabel Light) to be unattractive. Once again, we encounter the phenomenon that typefaces – regardless of their optical legibility – trigger particular feelings on the part of readers simply through their appearance, and can have a positive or negative impact. This seems to be pragmatic evidence to show that, over and above their primary and essential task of acting as a visual means of transport for language, typefaces are also able to communicate atmosphere.

In this context, Spencer mentions analyses by Ovink and Zach-risson that reinforce this assumption. However, on the basis of an analysis of advertisements over a period of 50 years, Spencer believes 'that findings of congeniality may have little temporal stability, and such an examination supports Warde's view, that the choice of an appropriate typeface is a subconscious act, the effect of which is ephemeral. We may also reflect that sanserif letterforms which have been much used in this century to express the notion of "modernity" were first revived in the eighteenth century because of their associa-tions with rugged antiquity.'

In Kapr's opinion: 'The choice of typeface is naturally decisive for the interpretation of a text and its content. It is also permissible to interpret a text in various ways, much as an opera or a piece of music will be differently interpreted by different artists. But an artist working thus, with an existing work, must take care to reflect the spirit of the work; he may not work against it.'

Willberg reproduces the poem 'Bildhauerisches' by Christian Morgenstern from five different editions, and points to the 'interac-tion of text and type (and typographic design, for type size, arrange-ment and emphasis all have their effect)'. After analysing the five ver-sions, he concludes that 'the poem can be read in all five versions. If we nevertheless feel (despite the reduction in size) that it does not remain unaffected by the type, then this is an indication that the design of the type is also absorbed in the reading of the text, and

Typography may be defined as the art of rightly disposing printing material in accordance with specific purpose; of so arranging the letters, distributing the space and controlling the type as to aid to the maximum the reader's comprehension of the text. Typography is the efficient means to an essentially utilitarian and only accidentally aesthetic end, for enjoyment of patterns is rarely the reader's chief aim. Therefore, any disposi-

Typographie kann umschrieben werden als die Kunst, das Satzmaterial in Übereinstimmung mit einem bestimmten Zweck richtig zu gliedern, also die Typen anzuordnen und die Zwischenräume so zu bestimmen, dass dem Leser das Verständnis des Textes im Höchstmaß erleichtert wird. Die Typographie hat im Wesentlichen ein praktisches und nur beiläufig ein ästhetisches Ziel; denn nur selten will sich der Leser vornehmlich an ei-

Typografie kan omschreven worden als te zijn de kunst van op een juiste wijze drukmateriaal te ordenen in overeenstemming met een bepaald doel; van zodanig de letters te rangschikken, de ruimte te verdeelen, en het schrift te beheersen, als nodig is om zo volledig mogelijk het goede verstaan van de tekst door de lezer te bevorderen. Typografie is het doeltreffende middel tot een in wezen nuttig, en slechts bij gelegenheid

La typographie peut se définir comme l'art d'optimiser la disposition de l'écrit imprimé en fonction de sa destination spécifique; celui de placer les lettres, de répartir l'espace et de choisir les caractères afin de faciliter au maximum la compréhension du texte par son lecteur. L'aspect esthétique de la typographie n'est, en fait, qu' accidentel; son but est essentiellement utilitaire, car l'agrément d'une belle présentation n'est que rare-

La tipografia può essere definita l'arte di saper disporre esattamente il materiale da stampare in funzione di un scopo specifico; quindi l'arte di saper posizionare le lettere, distribuire lo spazio o controllare il disegno dei caratteri al fine di aiutare il lettore ad avare la migliore comprensione del testo. La tipografie è il mezzo efficiente per un utilizzo essenziale e solo occasionalmente il godimento estetico delle forme diventa lo scopo prin-

71   Same typeface, same type size, same width of line, same linespacing; nevertheless, the blocks of text look different, because each language has a unique text-image.

A Missal was printed at Cologne in 1483, and the textura faces cut for it were given exaggerated terminals, in some texts diamond-shaped in others horizontal, which make them dazzling and rather ugly. At the same time, about 1465–80, the types of the basic book-script fashion give way in the books of scholastic philosophy and law to condensed types with the fractured curves and

A Missal was printed at Cologne in 1483, and the textura faces cut for it were given exaggerated terminals, in some texts diamond-shaped in others horizontal, which make them dazzling and rather ugly. At the same time, about 1465–80, the types of the basic book-script fashion give way in the books of scholastic philosophy and law to condensed types with the fractured curves and emphatic terminals of the

A Missal was printed at Cologne in 1483, and the textura faces cut for it were given exaggerated terminals, in some texts diamond-shaped in others horizontal, which make them dazzling and rather ugly. At the same time, about 1465–80, the types of the basic book-script fashion give way in the books of scholastic philosophy and law to condensed types with the fractured curves and emphatic terminals

A Missal was printed at Cologne in 1483, and the textura faces cut for it were given exaggerated terminals, in some texts diamond-shaped in others horizontal, which make them dazzling and rather ugly. At the same time, about 1465–80, the types of the basic book-script fashion give way in the books of scholastic philosophy and law to condensed types with the fractured curves and empha-

A Missal was printed at Cologne in 1483, and the textura faces cut for it were given exaggerated terminals, in some texts diamond-shaped in others horizontal, which make them dazzling and rather ugly. At the same time, about 1465–80, the types of the basic book-script fashion give way in the books of scholastic philosophy and law to condensed types with the fractured curves and emphatic terminals of the textura, as in one used by

72   Each typeface gives the same text a new appearance and represents it somewhat differently. P. 56, from top to bottom: 8.5/12.5 pt Caecilia Roman; 10/12.5 pt Monotype Baskerville Roman; 9.5/12.5 pt Collis Roman; 9/12.5 pt Linotype Univers 430 Basic Regular; 11/12.5 pt Trinité No 2 Roman Condensed. P. 57, from top to bottom: 9/12.5 pt

A Missal was printed at Cologne in 1483, and the textura faces cut for it were given exaggerated terminals, in some texts diamond-shaped in others horizontal, which make them dazzling and rather ugly. At the same time, about 1465–80, the types of the basic book-script fashion give way in the books of scholastic philosophy and law to condensed types with the fractured curves and emphatic terminals of the

A Missal was printed at Cologne in 1483, and the textura faces cut for it were given exaggerated terminals, in some texts diamond-shaped in others horizontal, which make them dazzling and rather ugly. At the same time, about 1465–80, the types of the basic book-script fashion give way in the books of scholastic philosophy and law to condensed types with the fractured curves and emphatic terminals of the textura,

A Missal was printed at Cologne in 1483, and the textura faces cut for it were given exaggerated terminals, in some texts diamond-shaped in others horizontal, which make them dazzling and rather ugly. At the same time, about 1465–80, the types of the basic book-script fashion give way in the books of scholastic philosophy and law to condensed types with the fractured curves and emphatic ter-

A Missal was printed at Cologne in 1483, and the textura faces cut for it were given exaggerated terminals, in some texts diamond-shaped in others horizontal, which make them dazzling and rather ugly. At the same time, about 1465–80, the types of the basic book-script fashion give way in the books of scholastic philosophy and law to condensed types with the fractured curves and emphatic

A Missal was printed at Cologne in 1483, and the textura faces cut for it were given exaggerated terminals, in some texts diamond-shaped in others horizontal, which make them dazzling and rather ugly. At the same time, about 1465–80, the types of the basic book-script fashion give way in the books of scholastic philosophy and law to condensed types with the fractured curves and emphatic terminals of the

Lexicon No 2 Roman A; 9.5/12.5 pt ITC Officina Sans; 10.5/12.5 pt Monotype Bembo Roman; 10/12.5 pt Scala Sans Regular; 10.5/12.5 pt Adobe Garamond Regular. These two pages also show the relative importance of size designations: what looks about the same size visually varies in designation between 9 and 11 pt.

contributes its own tone to the overall music, either constructively or negatively. It also becomes apparent that harmony is indispensable. The conclusion must be that good typographers are right to give serious consideration to which typeface they choose for which text.'

When Willberg remarks (even if only in parentheses) that it is not the typeface alone, but also the typographic design – type size, arrangement, emphasis – that is responsible for the overall atmosphere or impression, he touches, in my view, on a key point.

The impression created by any one typeface can only be assessed when all the typefaces concerned are used to set the same text, in the same size, to the same measure, with the same linespacing, and are printed by the same method, with the same ink and inking, on the same paper, with the same margins.

Any change to any one of these elements changes the impression created by the type, for they are all interrelated [71, 72]. In a book, for instance, the individual elements are also more or less closely related to its extent and to its stability or flexibility, and thus to the way it is bound and the binding materials – that is, to its haptic nature, its physicality.

A theoretically less attractive typeface can, through the proper choice and skilful deployment of all the other elements, be so enhanced that, as part of a typographic whole, it hits the right note. For typographers, analyses of the impression created by typefaces are thus often purely theoretical: they neglect the sheer complexity of typographic practice. They also harbour the danger that their results may incline people to apply prescribed solutions. This is something that creative typographers guard against.

Notes

The following works have further and sometimes more extensive discussion of typographic detail:

JAN TSCHICHOLD, *Schriften 1925–1974*, 2 vols, ed. Günter Bose & Erich Brinkmann, Berlin: Brinkmann & Bose, 1991 & 1992.

ROBERT BRINGHURST, *The elements of typographic style*, 2nd edn, Vancouver: Hartley & Marks, 1996

FRIEDRICH FORSSMANN & RALF DE JONG, *Detailtypografie*, 2nd edn, Mainz: Hermann Schmidt, 2004

HANS PETER WILLBERG & FRIEDRICH FORSSMANN, *Lesetypografie*, 2nd edn, Mainz: Hermann Schmidt, 2005

P. 8   Saccades, regression saccades. NIELS GALLEY & OTTO-JOACHIM GRÜSSER, 'Augenbewegung und Lesen' in: HERBERT G. GÖPFERT et al (ed.), *Lesen und Leben*, Frankfurt a. M, 1975, p. 65. Quotations in this chapter are made from this essay. More recently Kevin Larson, working for Microsoft, has investigated legibility of text with typographic considerations in mind. Larson's article 'The science of word recognition' (July 2004) can be found on the Microsoft website: <http://www.microsoft.com/typography/ctfonts/WordRecognition.aspx>.

     'a ridiculous error'. JAN TSCHICHOLD, *Erfreuliche Drucksachen durch gute Typographie*, Ravensburg, 1960, p. 16.

10   'will neither be very "different" nor very "jolly"'. STANLEY MORISON, *First principles of typography*, 2nd edn, Cambridge, 1967, p. 8.

13   'alternative forms for some letters'. JOST HOCHULI, 'Magdeburg 1926–1932: Ein systematischer Schriftunterricht', *Typografische Monatsblätter*, March/April 1978, pp. 81–96.

14   'the French ophthalmologist Emile Javal'. EMILE JAVAL, *Physiologie de la lecture et de l'écriture*, Paris, 1905.

     'the simple form of a'. A similar picture was published in: JAN TSCHICHOLD, *Treasury of alphabets and lettering*, New York, 1966, p. 36. See also: MILES A. TINKER, *Legibility of print*, Ames, Iowa, 1963, p. 61. The book summarizes many years of scientific research into legibility. Among other its qualities, it has a valuable critical bibliography (238 items).

15   'optical facts'. Generally and for more detailed discussion, see: HILDEGARD KORGER, *Schrift und Schreiben*, Leipzig, 1972. – MICHAEL HARVEY, *Lettering design*, London, 1975. – Especially for the design of a typeface: ADRIAN FRUTIGER, 'Der Werdegang der Univers', *Typografische Monatsblätter*, January 1961, p. 9 ff.

18   'optical requirement'. For a detailed, also technical discussion of this problem, see: WALTER TRACY, *Letters of credit*, London, 1986, p. 32 ff.

20   'objective and subjective radiation'. PAUL RENNER, *Die Kunst der Typographie*, Berlin, 1939, p. 24 ff.: 'For each typeface has a characteristic series of different tones of grey, however black the printer's ink may be. Thin hairlines seem not just more delicate, but actually lighter in colour; all thick strokes seem not just laid on the paper with greater emphasis, but also darker, blacker. This effect can be explained in terms of "objective radiation" – determined by the nature of the light and the quality of the paper – and as "subjective radiation", determined by the nature of human percepti-

on. The white surface reflects all the light – but not, like a mirror, according to the angle of incidence of the rays that strike it. Rather it scatters the incoming light in all directions, according to the nature of this surface. … On any white surface there is also a mist of light, like the mist of water over asphalt during a heavy shower of rain. A black imprint will be lightened by the scattered light of objective radiation, from the edges inwards. The narrower the black-printed area is, the lighter it will be. Subjective radiation works in the same way, originated by the scattered light on the cornea of the eye and other properties of our human visual system. Thus it happens that a hardly measurable mistake in the width of a stroke is more disturbing in small sizes, or in mechanical reduction, than in larger sizes. And this is often only noticed in small sizes, because here the difference is less one of difference of width – that is, of quantity – but it appears more as a difference of colour, and is thus a matter of quality.'

TINKER, p. 32 ff.

'scriptura humanistica'. See the groundbreaking work of B. L. ULLMAN: *The origin and development of humanistic script*, Rome: Edizioni di Storia e Letteratura, 1960.

23 'text in capitals'. HERBERT SPENCER, *The visible word*, 2nd edn, London, 1969, p. 30.

26 'residual letterspace'. KORGER, p. 23.

27 'the need for equal light'. On the topic of the optical balancing of letterspaces: DAVID KINDERSLEY, *Optical letter spacing for new printing systems*, 2nd edn, London, 1976. However, Kindersley only discusses here the balancing of the spaces, without any consideration of whether they are equal – but too small, too large, or just right.

32 'length of the line'. Gill: 'not more than 12 words' [not more than 70 characters] (ERIC GILL, *An essay on typography*, London, 1931, p. 91). – Tschichold: 8–10 words [45–58 characters] (JAN TSCHICHOLD, *Typographische Gestaltung*, Basel, 1935, p. 38). – Ruder: 50–60 characters (EMIL RUDER, *Typographie*, [1967] Sulgen, 2001, p. 43). – Kapr: 50–60 characters (ALBERT KAPR, *Hundertundein Sätze zur Buchgestaltung*, Leipzig, 1973, p. 18). – Bringhurst: 45–75 characters (ROBERT BRINGHURST, *The elements of typographic style*, 2nd edn, Vancouver, 1996, p. 26). – Willberg/Forssman: 60–70 characters (HANS PETER WILLBERG & FRIEDRICH FORSSMAN, *Lesetypografie*, 2nd edn, Mainz, 2005, p. 17).

'reader preferences'. TINKER, p. 28.

35 Figure 40. Text by Hans Peter Willberg, in: FRIEDRICH FRIEDL (ed.), *Thesen zur Typografie: 1960–1984 / Theses about typography: 1960–1984*, Eschborn, 1985, p. 45.

44 'italic'. TINKER, p. 54.

47 'the interdependence'. TINKER, 88 ff.

'indenting'. Tschichold's main essay on this question is published in translation as 'Why the beginnings of paragraphs must be indented': JAN TSCHICHOLD, *The form of the book*, Vancouver, 1991, pp. 105–9.

49 Figure 66. Text by STANLEY MORISON: *First principles of typography*, p. 5.

50 Figure 67. Text by Hans Peter Willberg, in: FRIEDL, *Thesen*, p. 49.

51 Figure 68. Text is altered from Günter Gerhard Lange's words, in FRIEDL, *Thesen*, p. 32.

52 Figure 69. Text by Henri Friedlaender, in: FRIEDL, *Thesen*, p. 32.

Figure 70. Text from: ROY PORTER, *Enlightenment*, London, 2001, p. 332.

54 TINKER, p. 64.

SPENCER, pp. 29–30.

54 Kapr: ALBERT KAPR & WALTER SCHILLER, *Gestalt und Funktion der Typografie*,
    Leipzig, 1977, p. 128.
    Willberg: HANS PETER WILLBERG, *Buchform und Lesen* ('Beilage' to the Börsenblatt
    für den Deutschen Buchhandel [Frankfurt a. M.], no. 103/104, December 1977),
    pp. 8–9.
55 Figure 71. STANLEY MORISON wrote the original text for the entry on 'Typography'
    in the 12th edition of the *Encyclopedia Britannica* (Chicago & London, 1929). –
    German: *Grundregeln der Buchtypographie* (Bern, 1966) – Dutch: *Grondbeginselen
    der typografie* (Utrecht, 1951) – French: *Les premiers principes de la typographie*
    (Brussels, 1960) – Italian: in JOST HOCHULI, *Il particolare nella progettazione gra-
    fica* (Wilmington, 1987).
56 Figure 72. Text from: HARRY CARTER, *A view of early typography*, Oxford, 1969, p. 37.
58 WILLBERG. *Buchform und Lesen*, p. 8.

Other books in this series

Detail in typography belongs to a loose set of Hyphen Press paperbacks, which share the same small format, but which are otherwise different from each other in their design. All of the books are works that have been published before, in other languages or else on other occasions. These are books that have already proved themselves.

Gerrit Noordzij
  The stroke: theory of writing
This is the most concise and powerful statement of Gerrit Noordzij's theory of writing. Published in Dutch in 1985, this is the first English edition.

Robin Kinross
  Modern typography: an essay in critical history
The book redefines the subject of 'modern typography' in a long historical view, from 1700 to now. Published first in 1992, it is now available in a revised and updated edition.

Robin Kinross
  Unjustified texts: perspectives on typography
A particular view of typographic design is embodied in this gathering of articles from twenty-five years of writing about the subject. The pieces range from short reviews and notices to full-scale essays, notably 'Fellow readers'.

Norman Potter
  What is a designer: things, places, messages
Potter offers a high-level consideration of principles, fused with a down-to-earth discussion of how design work may actually be carried out. Published first in 1969, this fourth edition of the book brings it to an international readership.